DARK
to
LIGHT

STRUGGLE OF
A MANIC-DEPRESSIVE

JENNIFER TOTH

Olympus Story House

Contents

Dedication
Acknowledegement

Dedication

To my Mother who was always there for me.
Thank You Mom. Love You Forever.

Acknowledgement

For Lorraine, your faith and advocacy for my books and mental health in general blows me away. Thank you for keeping your faith and so inspiring me once again. So grateful for everything you are doing for my books! I am honored to have you rooting for me and my work. Your efforts leave me speechless. Thank you!

Freedom for the Words

Whatever drips down that's what I say—
I don't want to get in its way.
Imperfect in its perfection,
I just love its tell-tale intention.
On golden waves of glory's sky,
Of reaching low or reaching high,
Whatever may please its palate's taste
Fancy pleasures or treasure's waste.
For who am I to stop its rolling creation,
That stems from my being high above idle adulation?
Or to trample it with edits from my meager brain,
Who do I think I am to sit and re-arrange?
What silver shall fall down I shall pick up,
Be it tarnished or shining in its unique strut.
Be it simple or complex in its verse or its rhyme,
My goodness, whatever, it's genuinely mine!
My child, my children, I shall not cast you afar,
I shall embrace you and accept you just as you are—
Unique bright lights that sparkle my page,
Running little rascals, I shall always press save.
Sheer joyous wonder that you are even here,
For once I was so barren and all alone in my fear.
But now I collect you each word like breath,
And thank God, he sent you my birds of the nest.
So, come to me words and do not hold back be true,
For you are my life line, and without, what would I do?
My family, my family, my most treasured souls,
But unlike others I shall not make you walk on hot coals.
I shall let you breathe in the sunshine,
I shall let you dance in the rain,
I shall let you speak your whole mind,
You need not try and explain.
So come to me my children and tell me your tales,
Gather up your belongings for I've set you free from English jails.

On This Page

On this page,
I do not wish to spill my emotions out,
Yet they bleed from my fingertips as I bite my lips.
I do not wish to bare my soul,
Yet it leaps from within;
I have no such control.
I do not wish the dreams and schemes
Of my mind be known,
Yet they scream so loudly as outward they're thrown.
I do not wish to share my inner core,
Yet it glows and it breathes;
I can stop it no more.
Nothing is what I want to share,
Though thoughts ooze from my membrane,
My heart, and soul,
Demanding delivery.
Staring at this page I want to yell so loudly,
That the walls crumble around me,
Because I am in so much pain,
I am so very afraid, and my heart is broken in two.

Of Madness

Madness circles in
I am spinning in the darkness
Of my weary soul
And I am out of control
All thoughts fleeting
I have entered the other side
Where shadows show their faces
Where shadows do abide
I am becoming like them
I am retreating from the sun
I am leaving everything behind
I am on the run
From the madness that circles round
Will it catch me?
Will it vex me?
It's closing in again
Dark nights of the soul
Shedding of water untold
Still the darkness has its way
But I can't let it stay
Pinning me down
No way to get around
That madness that soaks my soul
Is coming in for landing
As my life is fading
By the blade
Of madness, darkness, and despair.

My Ride

My ride is full of dark things
It is full of holes
Stories are shared
While deep secrets unfold
There are despondents
The invisible sit
The heartbroken
There are no counterfeits
It is full of riches
Full of poor and wealthy hands
Full of opinions
Rooted from ego lands
Hope rises and falls
Light fades to dark
There is salvation
And dust turned to spark
Sometimes it's full of brightness
Goes smooth and straight
I've seen great healing
And change of fate
No one's a stranger to happiness
No one's a stranger to pain
Though we are all different
We all look the same
On my ride we are all on a journey called Life
Just trying to get through the days and the nights.

Can't Find My Way Home

Sickened to the point of death
I tremble the heat
And ride the light
Of valleys and peaks
Until I am no more.
The darkness has taken over
Leaving me a ghost of what I am
As I struggle for reason and sense
I can't find any except to say
This is the way—the way home.
Tripping and falling
Over snowflakes
I merge with the nighttime sky;
Black leather sky
And the whole while I am dying inside
And nobody knows it but me.
Sliding backwards I am a skeleton
Of what I once dreamt.
Dream and reality exist
Duality along different streets.
I never knew the sky could be so black
I think as my stomach groans in intervals
That only God can understand.
I shrink once more—
Caught in the web of blindness;
I am wrapped for burial,
And only God can save me
To help me find my way home.

Down on My Knees

I fall down pits of despair
A ladder is sent down
As I climb out, I realize
Everything is an upward climb.
I see my destiny
From the furthermost horizon
As I slip and slide
On the cobblestones of my mind.
I am down on my knees.
Dark blue freckled sky with stars
Is my backdrop and comfort
While dark shadows follow me
And I can't get away, no.
I run into the embrace of the moon
I hide from the tale telling sun
And no matter how hard I try
I can't get out of this spider web.
I am down on my knees.
I am awake in this darkness that surrounds
Eating me, mind, body, and soul
And I've nowhere to hide
And nowhere to go.
I stepped on a land mine of flowers
Was delivered up into the sun
Staring back down
I realized my work is not done.
I am down on my knees.
A mere passerby am I
On planet Earth
Heaven is my true home
Homesick, but not my time.
Restful sleep is what I need
Ah to search for some clean air to breathe
Like a brush fire I take off

To find some peace though I am lost
I am on the run from those who criticize
And from those who keep track
I am on the run from the monkey
That used to be on my back
I am down on my knees.
I need to breathe the fumes
To touch the illuminating flames
To feel the freeze of death
To know I am real and not insane
Deep blue sky full of lighthouses
Who are my only witnesses
As I am running down cobblestones of my life
Hiding from the shadows the suck my spirit
I am down on my knees.
One day I will be here no more
What can I tell you
All words being said
And actions done.
And for the last time, I am down on my knees
Paying homage to a God I adore.

Help

The truth courses through my veins
My eyes are lit up like flames
Hit for the last time
Fighting not to go insane
He said what you have here
Is a beautifully created Ivory mask
It has served you well
Over the years
But now it's time it cracked
The mask is chipping
And falling away
And all that I locked
Has come out to play
Cause I am on fire
I burn from within
With a rage forged in battles
That I always win
I wear purple hearts
I am a green beret
But today the mask has fallen
Pieces of marble lie
I fall in ruins
And land on my sword
The battles are over
With one final word
Help.

Hell or Heaven Sent

Swimming upstream
Against a strong current
As time stands still
I feel so lost and alone
Centered but falling
Standing but crawling
Seems I've got no place
To call my home
Rising and climbing
Not once looking back
Leaving no tracks
No others may know
For I have spied
The eyes of hell
I have seen the end
Of a rainbow
I see out of eyes
Of an old soul
And I've lived this
And breathed this before
In the end I wonder
What will my struggles prove?
What will break my chains
So tightly clasping me?
What will soothe my pain
When I am good and free?
When everything is spent,
Am I hell or heaven sent?

A Toast

Let's all drink a toast to personal evolution
Even if it makes us bleed,
I said, laughing with a wicked laugh
That even the devil couldn't conceive.
Another toast said I, this time to Freedom,
You know he's an old friend of mine,
And when he leaves, an invisible cell appears,
And we all start doing hard time.
The people stared, mouths wide open,
As I continued laughing with another toast,
This one's for good ole Peace of Mind,
You know what we need but can never find.
Hysteria hit me as my eyes glowed red,
And then one last toast I said.
This one's for Hope may it always have wings,
Though in all of my heart 'twas the deadest of things.
Still the people glared in horror,
At my maddening display,
But I just kept on laughing,
Straight up till the next day.

Visitor

Darkness trickles in—
My long-lost friend.
We sit amongst the campfire
Talking of old times
Long since gone by.
He asks me for a cigarette
So I give him my last one.
I ask him what he's doing here
He said just taking a break
So, he thought he'd come and visit
And bring me some more heartache.
His sharp nails glow crimson
In the deep midnight hour.
He can't help but cut me.
He can't help but leave a scar.
Still, what is that between old friends?
Looking down to add more wood, I noticed he had gone.
So, I sat and pondered his return,
In the stillness of my soul.

In the Passing

I am old in young skin
I don't remember when it all began
Details like movies roving my mind
Life is so unkind sometimes
Mixture of dark colors that stick and bind
Just a butterfly in the web
I can feel my wings detaching
I can feel the pain it brings
But I can't tell you anything
Except flowers in the moonlight
Wait maybe grasses in the rain
Or pink lightning flashing
I am afraid of everything
Can you paint me new life?
Can you make it sing?
Can you talk in riddles?
Do you know of darker things?
I like to keep the light on
I like walking in the rain
I like watching nature's movie
I am in love with everything
I am old in young skin
I can't remember when I began
I remember details of who I think I am
Just a butterfly without wings
I love to fly and I love change
Sometimes I take my thoughts out
Just to re-arrange
Will you show me your white soul?
Cause it's cold from where I've been
I've been shivering for years
Caught in a deep freeze
Staring out with child's eyes
I won't hurt or criticize

I feel the pain it brings
Deep blues for souls to sing
I am old in young skin
Reality covered up in neat illusion
Child eyes and kid fears
I am young in young skin
But I am old too
My tree rings are plenty
I can show you photographs
Etched in life
Stored in my mind
Taken at precise angles
Under different lights
I can show you pink lightning
We can walk in the rain
We can watch nature's movie
Sing blues for our pain
And color in bright colors
Where dark colors reign,
We can do all these things
So quickly, so fast
Just lend me your glance
And our memories will pass
It will be like butterflies
With bright wings
Flowers in the moonlight
Grasses in the rain
And maybe in that moment
I won't feel so very alone
So very alone
And so very insane.

Innocence

In the beginning
There was no end.
My vision extended
Far beyond
The furthermost horizon,
And continued on,
Into infinity,
Until it returned to me,
Smiling.
I stood,
A young pioneer
On a new land,
With hopes in one pocket
And dreams in the other.
In the beginning
The air was rich with faith
And I too,
Glowed its golden essence,
While love flowed throughout the land,
Filling mighty waterfalls,
With its melodic peaceful ways.
Yes, in the beginning,
Life was grand,
And I one amidst the masterpiece,
That filled the space,
I staked as my own.
I never saw the end coming,
It was never in my vision's eye,
Until one day unknown to me,
Dropped down a tear straight from my eye,
And landed on the masterpiece,
Dark colors formed I was surprised.
I knew a change had come to be,
And so the end I saw at last,
Out at a distance would come to pass.

Out at a distance would come to pass.
The tear it came from joy of heart,
Still tore my masterpiece apart.
So there I stood eyes opened like skies,
Full of new knowledge that everything dies.

Let My People Go

Paths of circles leave no traces
And in the daylight we scatter
Like wild birds in flight
Caught up in gusts of wind
And kind breezes
Found on rooftops
On branches high
Walking through dewy grass
Building up strand by strand
New nests
Sun sets
Dusk
Moon takes center stage
And like a tribe
Out there in the desert
Right foot chained to right foot
The circle dance has once again begun.
Heads high, heads low, hands clapping,
Jumping up and down
In a feverous frenzy we
Chant, holler, hoot, and yell.
Like a family
Together we pull each other around
Carrying each other around the circle before us
And as the fire reaches its peak
If you look really close,
You can see the water rolling down our faces
And if you look even closer
You might just see someone you know
All the while us chanting
Let my people go.

Footprints in a Circle

The chanting begins again,
Slow hums, slow strides,
Heads held up in hope,
Heads lowered side by side.
Along we go the dance that heals,
And the in-betweens,
Of chills and tales,
That would stare you down,
If per chance you locked an eye,
With one of the family members,
Going round and round,
Laughing, singing, hoping, dreaming.
Yeah, we all know why the caged bird sings.
Hearty bird caged with hopes of salvation,
Hopes for a better day and a better way.
Tonight amidst the campfire,
We all merge as one—
One hope, one sweat, one tear, one joy,
One prayer,
That one day we will meet for tea,
And not for the heavy task of moving the earth,
Under our swollen feet.
Tonight, around the campfire,
Sand is thrown inside,
And when there is no more fire left to see,
Gone are the members of our family—
As if it never took place.
For we work so very hard but we, we leave no trace.
Just footprints in a circle,
And they are eternal.

Eternal Prayer

Clouds of orange smoke
Chanting that the silence broke,
Souls connected glowing white,
A circle of one prayer singing into the night.
And no one missed a beat, or a step,
Nor a breath, nor a word,
All the while moving and shuffling in one divine accord.
And you could not stop the flow, no,
For it came from the inside and above,
It moved fast then slow,
All the while gaining peace,
Gaining strength,
Finally breaking through, one family,
Into the promised land of some kind of relief.
And the earth it shook,
And the trees they swayed,
Their eyes transfixed on purpose,
Of a higher cry of a higher need.
And the bells of salvation sounded sharply,
As the throes of hell receded,
The family carried on knowing the line must be crossed.
And then rest.
All the night praying, all the night giving,
Their blood and sweat,
Until the sun began to rise,
And like the clouds of orange smoke,
They disappeared from sight,
Leaving only as witnesses,
the whispers of their united prayer,
Filtered up to the very throne of God,
They prayed, "Let Our People Go, Sweet God",
"Let our chains come undone Oh Merciful One".
And if you listen really good,
You can still hear the family chanting,
For their prayer is eternal.

We Are Family

When the circle takes its last
Turn around the curve
I wonder what our hearts will ask
All beating frayed with nerves
And when the chanting has gone to silence
And all the work has been laid to rest
Every single one of our groaning
And glowing family members
Will surely know the earth did move
We did more than our very best
The healing begins in the silence
When the campfire is gone from sight
When night turns to rivers of brightness
The victory we labored for is given freely
And burdens lifted, we now stand light
One family, one sorrow turned into joy
Our souls now new and refined
Together we have survived this beastly test of weather
And we are stronger for it
Our bond is Sacred, Holy, and True
We are family, we are family,
A bond that cannot change nor ages tear or break
For, we are family.

Red Roses

I felt a gust of wind
Sailing through the air
And reaching out its arms
It enveloped me right there.
I found myself in a garden
Of roses in full bloom—
They spoke to me with power
Of which I never knew.
They spoke to me a peace,
Though they never said a word.
They spoke to me with beauty—
That transported me out of my world.
Then the gust of wind
Enveloped me again
Took me sailing through the air
And carried me home with roses left,
Despair.

My Vigil

I have been shipwrecked on the isle of life
I ran from the darkness straight into the light
Give me some rain
Give me some sunshine
Give me some flowers
Give me some real time
There are no boundaries
For those who believe
As I sit vigil staring at a solitary tree.
My light bulb has finally been lit
I am real no counterfeit
I have survived by the mighty hand of God.
I need to breathe, to hear, to see
I need your touch to make me whole
As I sit vigil staring at a solitary tree.
Let's turn the world upside down
And empty its pockets…
I have paid my dues
I have walked miles in my shoes
Spied the eyes of hell
But I'm not here to tell
I have stood alone
Before crossroads bare
Didn't know which to choose
Waiting for you there
Soaked in silence's voice
Lost in the sunshine
Caught up in the rays
A pocket full of memories
Leading me to this day
I am a flower whose time has come
Blooming and shaking into a red rose
I have talked with a raven who knew
That life is precious and priceless too
As I sit vigil staring at a solitary tree.

As I sit vigil staring at a solitary tree.
I am a lighthouse bathed in lights untold
I am a book where mysteries unfold
I am like the burning sun
I am like the raging moon
Each night and day
A different bloom
My journey has been hard and long
And this is my song, my song
As I sit vigil staring at a solitary tree
My life unravels beginning to end
So I just smile and pretend
That I know what I am doing
Cause living in the light
Is new to me my friend.

My Life

Notes play on the harp in my soul
As I walk in between the raindrops
And finger paint on the brick wall
Of redemption
Running straight into the arms of eternity
There is no going back I am told
I have lived in a drop of dew
And I have lived in a hive of bees
I have lived in a robin's nest
I have lived in a forest of trees
I shower with flowers
That shimmers with rhyme
That glistens with life
Out of space and time
I have fought with a rose
I have chased a daffodil
I have run after a pansy
Just for the thrill
There is no going back I am told
Still, I have stained glass windows on my mind
And Church bells ringing telling me it's time
I hear the soundtrack of my life
In nature's scene
With each step that I take
It's like a dream
But it's all of my own making
If you know what I mean
For I have painted in bright colors
Where dark ones did reign
And every time I see some
I do the same
It's an amazing journey I like to call my life.

I Climb

Like the sun rising,
Like the baby turtles running towards a new shore,
Like a new stem pushing up through dewy ground,
Like a rainbow rolling down a dark storm,
I climb,
And like daybreaks new song,
I conquer familiarity,
I embrace rainstorms of individuality,
I struggle with fears of old,
Wearing them down with wet tears,
And thin telling scars,
And I climb,
With hopes and dreams,
Like each season comes and goes,
Up and down and ebb and flow,
High dips and low blows,
I climb,
Like everyone and everything else,
I climb.

Piece of Art

In the meadow of my soul,
Soft pink dogwoods grow,
And bloom and burst forth,
Giving light and light
So unfamiliar.
In the garden of my heart,
Treasures of blue pansies art,
Explode into masterpieces unknown,
I stand in awe of the entire thing.
In the ocean of my spirit,
Exists the rhythm of my being,
Intertwining with heart and soul,
Just leaving me reeling.
In the caverns deep in my mind,
Peace sits with happiness,
As red and yellow roses grow,
Mingling with my soul,
Taking pleasure in my heart,
Ignite my spirit to overflowing,
Yes indeed I am a piece of art.

Dreamer's Eyes

I see out of dreamer's eyes
Yellow colored glasses
And everything is sunny.
The dream begins with the moon,
And continues on with the sun,
As I am dancing to the beat
Of the Earth,
Rotating in its melodic trance,
I feel the desire,
It sets me on fire.
I dream of fields of daisies,
Gleaming in their brilliance,
Dressed in white robes,
Held together by yellow buttons.
I slide down the sun's rays
And land in a pile of rainbow leaves
That are newly fallen
And soft to the touch.
I plant the dreamer's seeds
And carefully await the harvest of gold.
My soul weeps for many,
Who are blind and cannot see,
The beautiful world around them
That I take delight in gleefully.
I am happiest when I am dreaming,
So please, shhh, don't wake me.

This is Life

In leaves turned
In sunlight noticed
In flowers seen
In river songs heard
This is where I lay my head
Gathering up the clouds above
Listening to the morning birds
It can't get better, I am told
There's a shake in my bones
There's a rattle in my brain
But soon I am so soothed
By the nature so untamed.
So, I am told and I listen
To a mockingbird so kind
He tells me I must linger
And to seek the Divine
I will not forgive you
If these sights you do not see
For in my darkest hours
They comforted me.
I am lost in the beauty that surrounds
I have become one with what I found
Last words to speak
In leaves turned
In sunlight noticed
In flowers seen
In river songs heard
This is Life, This is Life.

In a Day

Blooming forth as a Rose,
No thorns be seen—
For they are hidden with just cause!
The golden striped bumble bee is safe;
He brings forth Love giving Life!
The graceful Monarch, touched by orange,
Heavenly sent finds rest—
Upon Silky, Pearly Petals:
Glowing with Lightening White Illumination,
And sips Heavenly Dew; the Fountain of Youth!
Red cardinal glides on Golden Air,
And, with a momentary glance,
Greets a loving Hello,
That only Bee and Butterfly could meet,
In a foreign language which I, desired to know!
Red Cardinal, having no time for more,
On Mission sent by God,
Went off to collect both branch and string,
For a Palace he builds but for his Queen—
And I, invisible cloak I wore,
Have learned a Language so Sweet and Dear,
For I, Transfigured into White Rose,
To gather Mysteries of Foreign Tongue,
And as Red Cardinal flew away,
I Re-transfigured into the Sun!
But that is a story for another Day.

A Blessed One

When the troubles are all circling round,
When my Joy cannot be found,
When I search for my humor and it's lost in the gray,
When I feel a whole lot but got nothing to say,
That's when I have to take a step back,
Tell myself, this too shall pass, it can't stay.
When friends are as desolate as blue in a storm,
When pain is so hungry that my insides get torn,
When I want to laugh but I can just shed one tear,
When I'm running for light forever falling in fear,
That's when I have to take a step back,
Tell myself, this too shall pass, it can't stay.
When the sun is hot and my kite flies high,
When my friend is near underneath blue sky,
When the smiles come rolling and flowing with laughs,
When I thank God for living and saving me from the traps,
That's when I take a step back,
Tell myself, you're a blessed one, and thank God for this day.
When the breeze is firm and full of song,
When all my rights are never wrong,
When I am filled with peace and love,
When I am connected to God above,
I take a step back,
Tell myself, you're a lucky one, and
Thank the Lord things are this way.
So when the storms come calling all shaking with wrath,
And the darkness befalls me and I blocking its path,
Or if the sky is all filled with cottony clouds set on blue,
I'm just going to thank the Lord, yeah, that's what I'll do.
I'll take a step back and know that I'm a blessed one,
for what else can I say?

Cycle

Rainbow leaves
Spiral in animation
Towards the ground —
Sharing whispers
With the breeze,
And then,
Dying forever
Out of sound.
Beauty at its peak,
Closer to its death,
A moment
To rejoice its life,
Before its final breath.

Just Words

These are just words,
They don't mean any harm.
I whip them into shape,
When they step out of line.
I place them in position,
To create some order,
And sometimes they stay put,
While other times,
They break the border,
And roll out onto the floor,
Likemarbles they glide,
And I get down,
And pick them up,
To put them back inside.
Words are like children,
They need parameters,
Within which to play,
But they,
Never mean any harm,
Basically thoughts,
Like children just stray.
It's our responsibility,
To diffuse them,
If in fact,
Their intentions are ill,
Otherwise,
Let them flow,
As they will,
And they will surprise you,
With each sentence they inspire,
And before you know it,
They will have,
Set your page,
On fire.

www.ingramcontent.com/pod-product-compliance
Lightning Source LLC
Chambersburg PA
CBHW031241120626
46545CB00003B/1224